DARCY PUG PLAYS BASKETBALL

Megan Johnson McCullough, EdD

Illustrated by Alexis Eastburn

Charleston, SC
www.PalmettoPublishing.com

Darcy Pug Plays Basketball

First Edition

Hardcover ISBN: 979-8-8229-1581-7
Paperback ISBN: 979-8-8229-1582-4

Darcy Pug is the story of Megan's love for basketball. She began playing basketball in the 2nd grade on an all-boys' team. Megan still holds the records for most three pointers in a game, most three pointers in a career, and best free throw percentage for her high school called El Camino, in Oceanside, California. She earned a full ride scholarship to play basketball at Metro State in Denver, Colorado. Today, Megan still holds the individual game record at Metro State for free throw percentage. In this story, the character, Darcy Pug, is Megan and this name comes from Darcel McCullough, Megan's mother-in-law. The other pugs included in the story are all part of Megan's family. Coach Erin Butterfly is Megan's sister, Erin, and Assistant Coach Selena Caterpillar is Megan's sister-in-law, Selena. The players on the Monarchs include Megan's nieces, Sophia, Ruth, Tatiana, Lily, Becky, and Violet. Darcy's sister-in-laws, Portia, Laura, and Dereka are fans in the crowd watching the basketball game(s). Megan has always had pugs as pets and likes to name them after professional basketball coaches and players including Phil Jackson, Steve Nash, and Scottie Pippen. The ongoing theme of the butterfly representing the memory of Megan's mother, Rebecca Johnson, is again found in this story. A fun fact about Megan's father, Ray Johnson, is that he is the winningest boys' basketball coach at El Camino High School and in the entire state of California. Her husband, Carl, played basketball at El Camino for Megan's dad, and Carl Pug is the referee in this story.

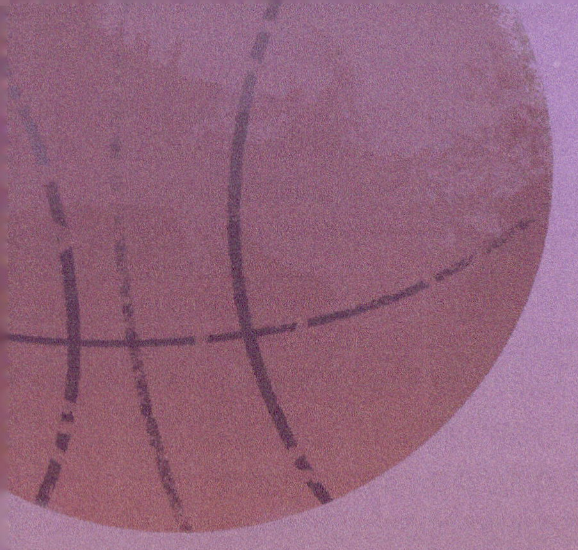

Darcy Pug loved to shoot hoops and dribble her basketball. She practiced her moves, tricks, and shots every single day before and after school.

Darcy Pug tried out for her school's basketball team called the Monarchs.

Coach Erin Butterfly and Assistant Coach Selena Caterpillar were very impressed by Darcy Pug's talent, so she made the team. Darcy Pug wanted her team, the Monarchs, to win their games.

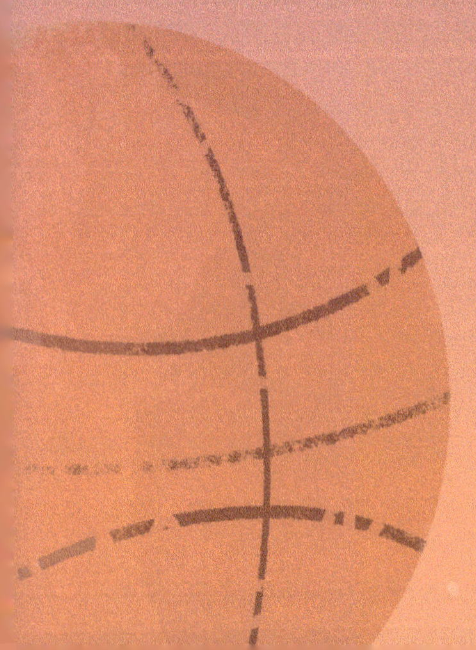

This meant that she and her team-mates Sophia Pug, Ruth Pug, Tatiana Pug, Lily Pug, Becky Pug, and Violet Pug, all had to work very hard together, learn the rules and plays, run to get faster, lift weights to get stronger, go to bed early, drink lots of water, and eat healthy meals.

When the Monarchs played their first game, the other Pugs were taller and bigger than they were. Coach Erin Butterfly and Assistant Coach Selena Caterpillar told them not to be scared, to play together, to have fun, and to trust in all their hard work.

02
05
CAPTAIN

Darcy Pug was voted the team captain, so she needed to be a leader for the team. When the Monarchs huddled up during a timeout, Darcy Pug said, "We can do this. I believe in each one of you. Try your best. Don't quit. We are a team."

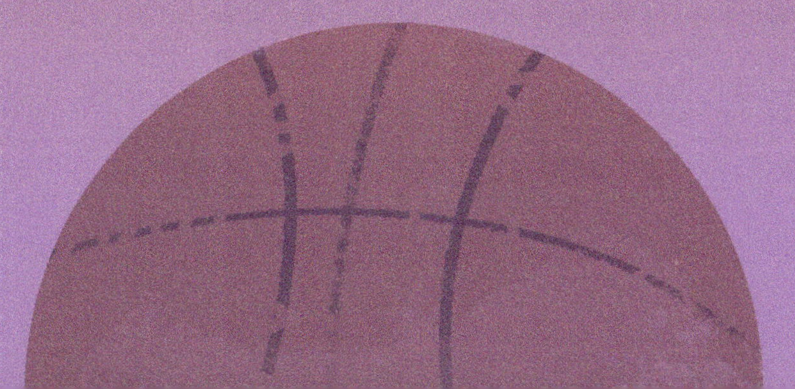

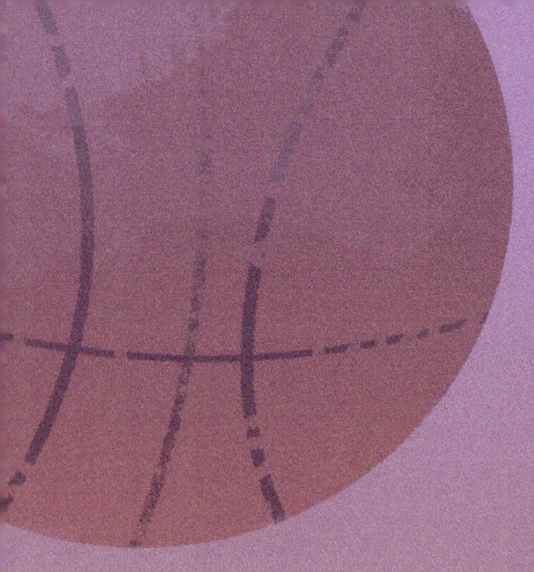

Because the Monarchs practiced their drills over and over again, gave each other high fives, and listened to their coaches, they won not only that first game, but the next 5 games in a row. They made it to the champion-ship game.

55 32
HOME VISTOR

WINNER
05
10
44

Every Pug was very, very nervous. This time Darcy Pug said to her teammates, "No matter if we win or lose, let's try to be the very best versions of ourselves out there". The Monarchs won the championship game 24 points to 23 points against the Mariposas.

The referee, Carl Pug, awarded the Monarchs with a giant trophy. All of the fans were yelling and cheering. Darcy Pug had a big smile on her face when she looked out at the crowd and saw her sisters, Portia Pug, Laura Pug, and Dereka Pug, all giving her a big thumbs up. After the game, the Monarchs made sure to tell the Mariposas that they played a good game.

NER

Being part of a team made Darcy Pug feel so happy and glad she decided to play basketball. Winning the championship game was not by luck. Darcy Pug had practiced and worked hard to make all her basketball dreams come true. Pugs like Darcy, never quit, always try their best, and help others be their very best too.

Basketball Skills

Shooting The Basketball

When you play basketball, you score points by shooting the ball through the basket. There are 3 places that points can be scored from. There is a big arc on the court that if you shoot behind it, the basket counts as 3 points. Anything you shoot inside the 3-point arc counts as 2 points. The last place you can shoot from is called the free throw line. When a player is fouled, they get to shoot from this line and each made basket counts as 1 point. This means you can either score 3, 2, or 1 point(s) when you play basketball.

Dribbling The Basketball

Whenever you have the ball, you have to dribble in order to move with it. You can only keep 1 hand on top of the ball and bounce it (with only 1 hand) when you move.

Dribbling Rules

You can only bounce the basketball with 1 hand at a time. If you bounce the ball with 2 hands it is called a "double dribble". If you bounce the ball then pick it up with 2 hands and bounce it again, this is also called a "double dribble". If you "double dribble" this is called a "turnover" and the other team will get the ball. When you dribble the ball and stop, you only get to move 1 step which is called a "pivot". You can step with 1 foot, but the other foot has to stay on the floor and not move. If you move the foot you don't step with, this is called "traveling". This is also another type of "turnover", and the other team gets the ball.

Pivot

If you are dribbling and stop, the only way to move is by doing a pivot. You can step with 1 foot and keep the other foot on the floor. You can turn in a circle rotating around the foot that stays on the floor.

Pass

You can pass the ball to another player a few different ways. Passing moves the ball around the court. You can either pass in the air straight to someone else which is called a "chest pass" or you can pass by throwing the ball so it bounces on the floor towards the player. This is called a "bounce pass". You can also take the ball up over your head and throw the ball to another player which is called an "overhead pass". When you pass, you can either use 1 or 2 hands to throw the ball.

Quarters 

There are 4 quarters in a basketball game. The first 2 quarters are called the 1st half and the 2nd - 2 quarters are called the 2nd half of the game. There is a break in the game called "halftime" which is between the 1st and 2nd halfs. Halftime gives the players a little break and lets the coaches talk to the players. Sometimes during halftime, there can be a show for the people watching the game to see while they wait for the 2nd half to start.

Offense

The team that is passing the ball or bouncing the ball and going in the direction of the basket to score points, is the team playing offense.

Defense 

The team without the ball that is trying to stop the ball, not let the other team score, and are trying to get the ball from the other team, is the team playing defense.

Foul 

When a player makes contact with the player who has the ball, this is called a foul. When you play defense, you can use your body to try to stop or get the ball from the other team, but you cannot touch other players to do this. Touching the other player(s), such as pushing or holding onto them, are examples of making contact and this is called a foul. When a foul happens, the player who made the contact is given 1 foul. After a player gets 5 fouls, they can no longer play in the game and have "fouled out". The number of fouls each player makes is added up to the total number of fouls the team has made. After the team has made 7 fouls, each foul that happens after means that the other team gets to shoot free throws. The number of team fouls starts over during the 2nd half of the basketball game.

Free Throw 

When a foul happens to the player with the ball who is shooting, the player shooting the ball gets to shoot free throws. If the player makes the basketball when they shoot and are fouled, they get to shoot 1 free throw which is called an "And 1". If the player gets fouled while shooting the basket but doesn't make the basket, they get to shoot 2 free throws. If the player is shooting behind the arc and gets fouled, they get to shoot 3 free throws. After 7 teams fouls, even when the player is not shooting when the foul is made, the player who was fouled gets to shoot "one-and-one" which means they might get to shoot 2 free throws. If they make the first free throw, they get to shoot 1 more free throw. This means the player can either score 1 or 2 points when they shoot free throws after 7 fouls. When the total number of fouls for the team is 10 or more, the player who is fouled gets to shoot 2 free throws no matter what. This means the player can either score 1 or 2 points depending on if they make both baskets.

Out of Bounds

A basketball court is shaped like a rectangle and there are lines that mark the perimeter. The player with the ball must stay inside the lines of the rectangle (court) otherwise they are "out of bounds". If you don't have the ball, you can step outside the lines. When the ball is passed or bounces outside the rectangle's lines, this is also out of bounds. The other team will be given the ball for offense if a player causes the ball to go out of bounds.

Referee

The referee is the person who makes sure the rules are being followed and decides when a foul or out of bounds has happened. This person wants to keep the game fair and safe.

Basketball Word Search

Find the following words and circle them:

BASKETBALL

COACH

DEFENSE

DRIBBLE

FOUL

OFFENSE

PASS

PIVOT

PLAYER

REFEREE

I	P	M	W	E	V	C	X	U	I	P	B
O	B	A	S	K	E	T	B	A	L	L	K
Z	C	M	E	Q	L	K	G	I	Z	A	R
R	Q	P	I	V	O	T	U	D	V	Y	W
F	T	W	S	A	O	B	N	L	U	E	C
C	O	A	C	H	M	I	E	Q	Z	R	P
R	Q	X	Y	P	S	N	M	B	P	C	E
V	D	U	M	T	P	O	B	Q	A	B	U
U	R	A	T	D	E	F	E	N	S	E	B
W	I	S	U	X	H	F	M	B	S	A	D
Q	B	D	P	E	O	E	B	J	H	M	K
I	B	G	S	I	F	N	Q	H	S	T	V
B	L	H	P	H	P	S	V	F	O	U	L
Z	E	O	V	A	L	E	I	K	B	L	O
X	P	R	E	F	E	R	E	E	Y	F	P
N	T	A	P	O	G	M	Z	G	C	R	D

PHOTO Search

Circle every single basketball and every single pug
you see in the pictures below.

How many basketballs did you circle?

How many pugs did you circle?

COLORING ACTIVITY

Do your best to color in between the lines just like you would stay in between the lines of the basketball court

FILL IN THE BLANKS

Fill in the missing letter of these words

B_SK_TB_LL

DEF_NS_

DR_B_L_

_OUL

O_FEN_E

P_S_

PI_ _T

PLA_E_

RE_E_EE

10 SKILLS KIDS DEVELOP FROM PLAYING SPORTS

1. Teamwork skills - When kids play sports that have teammates, they learn to work together with other kids. They learn that each teammate is important in order for the practices and games to take place. Kids learn to communicate, cooperate, encourage, and help the other kids they are playing the sport with.

2. Physical activity skills - Kids learn various sport related skills to include running, passing, throwing, shooting, kicking, dribbling, and the different techniques to perform these skills. Kids also learn how to improve their speed, agility, quickness, and the proper form required for these skills.

3. Adversity skills - Kids learn the lessons associated with winning and losing, how to work through a challenge(s), and how to play with others who have different (equal to, better or worse) skills than themselves. Sometimes kids will be presented with drills or skills they don't grasp at first and learn they need to practice them to get better. Sometimes kids will play against teams that are very advanced and they will learn about motivation to improve so that they perform better against these teams.

4. Social skills - Sports require communication with teammates and coaches. Kids must learn how to speak to others to be able to play the sport together. They will learn how to communicate to work together, how to overcome challenges, and how to encourage/ support one another.

5. Time management skills - Kids learn that practices and games take place at specific times. A set schedule requires waking up on time, making sure to include time needed to travel to the practices and games, and making sure homework, chores, and tasks are done when they need to be done in order to have time to play sports.

6. Self-care skills - Kids learn they must stay healthy, injury free, eat at the right times, be rested, and pack all their equipment to play their sport. They need water, possibly sunscreen, the right safety equipment (such as a helmet or shin guards) and should bring a sweatshirt/sweater if it's cold. They also will learn to be sure their clothes/ uniform are washed and clean to wear.

7. Academic skills - Kids learn the rules of the sports which might involve how to keep score, strategizing, and/or designing plays. They will want develop understanding for what angles to shoot a basketball from, to kick a soccer ball from, or to hit balls from, etc. Understanding how a sport is played is a type of learning too.

8. Healthy habits skills - Kids learn they need to eat healthy, drink water, and get plenty of sleep to have the energy to play sports. Being hungry, thirsty, or tired means you won't feel good and you won't be able to give good effort. Plus, kids learn they want to avoid being sick so they can be at all the practices and games. This means they need to practice good hygiene and wash their hands regularly.

9. Planning skills - Kids need to have their practice/game clothes ready when needed, bring water, and make sure their homework and/or chores are complete based on having a practice/game coming up. There is a schedule of practices and games to be aware of which lets kids understand that you have to plan ahead to be organized so everyone knows what to do and where to be. Kids become aware that their parent(s)/ guardian(s) also must plan for the upcoming practices/games.

10. Self-efficacy skills - This is the belief kids develop in themselves while playing the sport. Kids learn about their personal strengths and weaknesses when it comes to playing a specific sport. They may feel confident and talented, become aware they need to practice and/or improve at the sport, and/or may realize a particular sport(s) is not suitable for them. They may decide to try to excel at one sport or to choose another sport(s) to try.

Photo credits:
Ben Yosef, International Physique League
Kathy Magerkurth, Oceanside Photographics Studio
Lorenzo Gaspar, AAU/ICN
Samantha Wallace, Every BODY's Fit client
Shannon Lopez, Every BODY's Fit client
Sonja Hults Photography

Answer Key

Photo Search

Basketballs - 8

Pugs - 9

Basketball Word Search

											P	
	B	A	S	K	E	T		B		A	L	L
											L	
		P	I	V	O	T					A	
											Y	
C	O	A	C	H							E	
									P		R	
	D					O			A			
	R		D	E	F	E	N	S	E			
	I				F			S				
	B				E							
	B				N							
	L				S	F	O	U	L			
	E				E							
	R	E	F	E	R	E	E					

FILL IN THE BLANKS

BASKETBALL

DEFENSE

DRIBBLE

FOUL

OFFENSE

PASS

PIVOT

PLAYER

REFEREE

To connect with Dr. McCullough you can find more information about her here:

Website: https://www.everybodysfitoceanside.com
Instagram @dr.megan_everybodysfit
Facebook: https://www.facebook.com/meganjohnson.374549
YouTube: https://www.youtube.com/fitlifeeverybodysfit
Amazon: https://www.bit.ly/MeganJohnsonMcCullough
Linktree: https://linktr.ee/everybodysfit
Linked In: www.linkedin.com/in/megan-johnson-mccullough-1b603a80